GW01564180

Learning from Rel

Just a Thought

Exploring Religious Ideas

Dave Francis

Hodder & Stoughton
A MEMBER OF THE HODDER HEADLINE GROUP

ACKNOWLEDGEMENTS

The publishers would like to thank the following for permission to reproduce copyright material in this volume:

Darton, Longman & Todd for extracts from *Moment of Christ: The Path of Meditation*, John Main OSB; Random House for extracts from *Roots*, Alex Haley; HarperCollins for an extract from *The Dark Face of Reality: A Study of Emergent Awareness*, Martin Israel. Scriptures from the *Good News Bible* published by The Bible Societies/HarperCollins Publishers Ltd, UK © American Bible Society, 1966, 1971, 1976, 1992, with permission.

Every effort has been made to trace and acknowledge ownership of copyright. The publishers will be glad to make suitable arrangements with any copyright holders whom it has not been possible to contact.

Illustrations by Geoff Chambers

The publishers would also like to thank the following for permission to reproduce copyright illustrations in this volume:

Dan Addelman p37 (bottom); Allsport/Tony Duffy p45; Andes Press Agency/Carlos Reyos-Manzo p32; Associated Press/Topham p12 (J. Silva), 26(David Giles), 45; Bridgeman Art Library p36, 39, 40; Corbis-Bettmann/UPI p33; Format/Raissa Page p43; Robert Harding Picture Library/Warren Faidley p25; Impact/Tom Webster p34; Kobal Collection p17; Yorkshire Sculpture Park, cover photograph: Andy Goldsworthy – 'Horse Chestnut Patch green to yellow torn leaves with spit, Yorkshire Sculpture Park, 24 October 1987'. All other photographs were supplied by the author.

The author would like to thank Deirdre Burke, Umar Hegedus, the Guru Nanak Nishkam Sewark Jatha Gurdwara, Ajahn Jayasaro and Punnadhammo Bhikkhu.

For Denise

British Library Cataloguing in Publication Data

Francis, Dave
    Just a thought
    Exploring religious ideas. – (Learning from religion)
    1. Religion – Juvenile literature   2. Religions – Juvenile literature
    I. Title
    291

ISBN 0 340 643684

First published 1996
Impression number   10 9 8 7 6 5 4 3 2 1
Year   1999 1998 1997 1996

Typeset by Litho Link Ltd, Welshpool, Powys, Wales.
Printed in Great Britain for Hodder & Stoughton Educational, a division of Hodder Headline Plc, 338 Euston Road, London NW1 3BH by Cambus Litho, East Kilbride.

CONTENTS

FOR THE TEACHER

It may seem odd, at a time when thematic mish-mash RE has come in for a lot of criticism, to be producing another thematic style RE textbook. Some of the criticism has been justified. Some themes have not been well chosen. Some thematic work has lacked substance or taken religious material 'out of context'. Other thematic work has fallen into the trap of attempting to summarise the 'essential' features of a religion, thereby providing only a narrow view of the religion in question.

The intention in RE is not primarily to instruct the pupils in the doctrine of any particular religion, denomination or sect. That is a task for those groups and their own religious and educational services. Teaching about doctrine may form a part of RE in state schools, but the primary task here must be to help pupils to gain inner strength – spiritual strength – to cope with life's difficulties and to make the very best of their lives. How are they to do this unless they know and understand something of the world's great religious and philosophical traditions? This is the real stuff of religious education and of the spiritual quest.

RE is not just for the religious. It is for all those concerned with life's meaning. Nor does it exclude the possibility that the best ways forward may lie outside religion.

The 'themes' in this book are not arbitrarily chosen. Rather, they relate to particular areas of religious concern; in this case the metaphysical and phenomenological issues for which pupils around key stage 3 show considerable interest. Is there a life after death? Is it possible to see into the future? Are there great spiritual as well as physical laws at work in the universe? How can we make best use of our senses to explore the meaning of life? With whom can we best explore these questions?

The selection of material made here attempts to do justice both to the context in which the material was originally set and to the various meanings and interpretations given by the religious traditions themselves. It is a tall order and no doubt there are failings along the way. Nevertheless, the concern has always been to help young people to make progress in their understanding of some of life's mysteries and to help them meet some of life's challenges with just a little more wonder, openness, sensitivity and moral courage. And if not with these attitudes, then perhaps with just a little more thought.

Thus, the chapters of this book are linked by the question of how the human mind relates to the 'Beyond'.

EXERCISES IN SILENT REFLECTION

Silent reflection exercises are used to help open up the experiential dimension of the topics being studied.

The basic preconceptions of this approach are as follows:

1   Religious Education is at least partly about helping people face themselves in the real world.

2   Spirituality may be manifested in progressive loss of self-concern, but can start with greater understanding of feelings.

3   Spiritual development involves commitment to do one's best.

4   Spiritual development involves a willingness to keep disruptive thoughts away and to keep the mind at rest on the job at hand.

5   Spiritual development involves physical, mental and emotional harmony.

6   Different religions may have their own ideas on how best this harmony is to be developed.

7   Silent reflection, or meditation, which finds a place in most religious traditions, may be one way, perhaps a very important way, in which spiritual progress may be made.

8   Reflection should not be ego-centred. It is not an escape, but aids progress towards calm alertness.

9   The development of good relationships is facilitated by the kind of quiet commitment that silent reflection can encourage.

10 Is there a life after death? If, as many religious believers say, there is an afterlife, then perhaps silent reflection can help a person prepare for this too!

General Aims of the silent reflection exercises used here.

1   To get in touch with ourselves.

2   To find, experience and expand our capacity for peace, healing, and wholeness.

3   To appreciate what lies beyond ourselves; perhaps to the very sources of being.

4   To focus on those ideas and values which help us know and accept ourselves, and from there see ways towards the quiet commitment and alertness which fosters caring relationships, even with those whom society appears to reject in some way.

5   To develop skills of attention and concentration.

6   To progress towards a harmony of body, mind and spirit. To gain or regain a sense of personal wholeness.

7   To discover the place and value of silence in daily living.

8   To help clarify our conception of the world and our place in it.

Finally, here is a story which acts as a general health warning for looking too deeply into the meaning of things.

A Zen Master was approaching death. It was the custom that when a great teacher was about to die he would write a koan for his pupils as a final thought and help towards their own enlightenment. One Master, for example, had written the word, 'dreams'. Meditating on this word, one of his disciples became instantly enlightened.

On this occasion, however, the Master refused to write anything. Disappointed, his disciples pleaded with him to write something before he passed away. Eventually he gave in and wrote, 'I don't want to die'.

The Master's disciples pondered on this phrase. Surely, they thought, an enlightened being such as their Master would not be afraid of death? Dissatisfied, they returned to the Venerable teacher and begged him to write another koan as they could not understand the first one.

Eventually the Master submitted to their pleas and wrote again. Excited, the pupils picked up the Master's note. It read, 'I **really** don't want to die'.

TAKING CARE WITH SILENT REFLECTION EXERCISES

Pupils should not be 'forced' to participate directly in exercises of silent reflection: they are essentially voluntary activities. One might still expect them to be silent, however, to allow others to participate.

Take care in preparing your own exercises not to put forward only one side of a controversial issue, and to explain any bias in particular exercises. If an exercise is being used which is distinctive of a religion or belief system, its source should be acknowledged.

Be prepared to follow up particular concerns and requests of individual pupils.

Pupils should be told to cease an exercise if they find themselves becoming frightened, emotional or if headaches begin.

The reflective activities used in this book take two main forms:

a) **Guided** e.g. 'Imagine you are 100 years old and you are looking back on your life.'

b) **Focused** on a single thought or word or item. e.g. repetition of a chosen mantra: 'Peace' or 'Maranatha'.

COVER PHOTOGRAPH

The cover photograph depicts a leaf sculpture by Andy Goldsworthy. This is an example of a style of modern art interested in the fleetingness of life. The photograph is the only record of this piece of art which, like much of life, is 'here today and gone tomorrow'. This sort of art shows that such fleeting moments can be beautiful, can remain in the memory, but can never be exactly reproduced. It also shows how human beings can work with nature and even attempt to 'improve' on nature. The result is something which may stimulate the human imagination and teach us something about what is important in life.

Introduction

THINK AGAIN!

Sometimes life is not what it seems. What seems clear at first may turn out to be something completely different on closer examination. This book explores some of the mysteries of the human mind. How do our senses relate to the world around us? What is the best way of thinking about the past and the future? Where does thought come from? Where does it go? And what can we do about it anyway? Think on!

1
PUZZLES AND MYSTERIES

Face Value

At first glance the computer generated design opposite looks like a colourful pattern. But look deeper. Relax your eyes and look through the picture, as though you were looking at something a bit further on. Perhaps you will see something other than the pattern on the surface. Don't try too hard. If nothing happens after a couple of minutes, leave it and maybe try again later. It doesn't matter if you can't see anything in the picture; lots of people can't get the hang of it, including some of your teachers. With practice you'll get there. It shows that, for one thing, there's more to life than meets the eye. We don't have to take everything and everyone at face value. There are often hidden depths. Take the people you meet every day for instance. There is more to people than their general appearance.

Much of what you do in this book is about looking deeper and further. The information exercises are designed to help you look beyond your first impressions. It's easy to write off things that are new, different or strange. But if you can get past that stage and investigate further there may be solutions to a lot of these puzzles and mysteries.

Stop for a moment . . . think of a person you have got to know in the last year. Do you remember your feelings towards them when you first met? What have you learned about that person since?

This book will introduce you to some religious people. Some you will have heard of, others will be

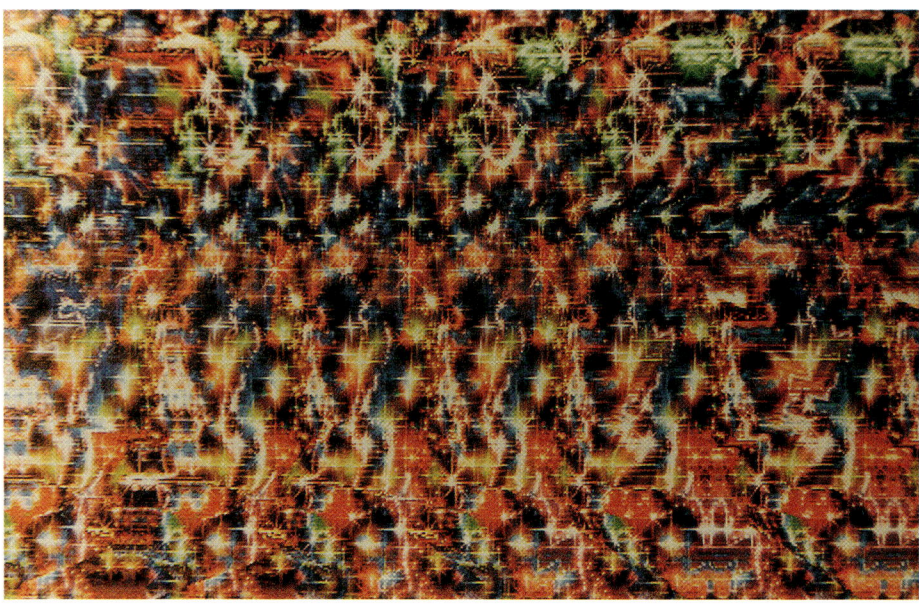
Tetrahedral Star, by Shiro Nakayama

new to you. Just remember; first impressions may not be the best idea of what people are like. Try to look deeper. It may help you understand yourself a little better too.

THINGS TO DO

1 Team up with one or two people who have a birthday close to yours. Each person should take a turn talking about themselves for 30 seconds. Try to remember what they tell you and then repeat back to them what you heard.

2 Make a list of puzzles and mysteries such as: is there a God? Are there such things as ghosts?

3 Choose ONE of these puzzles or mysteries and
(a) explain what the mystery is and
(b) say how you think it may be explained.

Mysteries in Science and Psychology

OK, HOW DO YOU EXPLAIN THE MYSTERY THAT HYDROGEN AND OXYGEN GASES DRAWN TOGETHER BY GRAVITATIONAL FORCES COMBINED TO PRODUCE A CONCENTRATED MASS OF INFINITE TENSION WHICH IN TURN PRODUCED A POWERFUL EXPLOSION KNOWN AS THE **BIG BANG**...

Will science one day solve all the mysteries in the universe? Here's a secret – promise not to tell anyone! It's already been done . . . in theory, at least!

Such is the power of modern science that as soon as a new mystery is discovered, a scientific theory is produced to solve it. Of course, the theory may prove wrong, but at least the mystery has a possible explanation. We will believe it until a better theory comes along.

There are still disputes of course. Scientists often disagree about which theory best fits the available evidence. This makes things complicated.

Stop for a moment . . . Would you like to be involved in such debates about science? Or do you prefer to let others deal with such mysteries? How do you feel about Mathematics and Physics? What are your feelings based on?

There are other mysteries, however, which seem to go beyond our universe.

Questions about the existence of ghosts or of God seem to go out of the reach of scientists. Such mysteries go beyond what can be measured or tested by observation.

Take the case of Hamish Grey, for example. Hamish was taken ill and rushed to hospital. In the operating theatre he became aware of the consultant saying, 'Pity you were too late'. Then he had an 'out of body' experience. He felt himself travelling along a tunnel and emerging into light. There were mind-blowing shapes and colours and a voice inviting him in. But Hamish decided he wasn't ready and travelled back down the tunnel to reawaken his 'dead' body, much to the surprise of his doctors.

Evidence of life after death? Or hallucinations caused by lack of oxygen to the brain? What had happened to Hamish's mind/spirit when he 'died'?

THINGS TO DO

1 With a partner discuss your reaction to these words: science; mystery; mathematics; physics; psychology; puzzle; ghosts.

2 (a) How do you think Hamish Grey felt about life when he recovered?

(b) Do a drawing of what Hamish Grey 'saw' during his out-of-body experience.

Looking at Evidence – The Resurrection of Jesus

Here are a couple of pages about what may be the world's greatest mystery – the claimed resurrection of Jesus.

There are at least two lots of stories about this mystery. One set of stories tells how the tomb in which Jesus was buried was found to be empty by his friends a couple of days after his execution. The other stories are about the appearances the Risen Jesus made to various people before he finally left the world to be with God.

Think about the empty tomb first. Many people have tried to solve the mystery of the empty tomb. But perhaps they are missing the point. What matters most for Christians, it seems, is not *what* happened, but that *something* happened. Take a look at these summaries of part of the empty tomb story. Remember, the body of Jesus, badly beaten, crucified and speared through the side, had been hastily buried on Friday evening, before the start of the Jewish Sabbath.

The Empty Tomb – by John (see *John* 20)

The empty tomb was discovered by Mary Magdalene early Sunday morning. She immediately contacted the disciples of Jesus. Two of them, Simon Peter and one other, (probably John himself) ran to the tomb and confirmed Mary's story. All they found in the tomb was the shroud in which the body of Jesus had been wrapped. The disciples then went home, already convinced that something amazing had happened.

The Empty Tomb – by Mark (see *Mark* 16)

Early on Sunday morning three women, Mary Magdalene, Mary the mother of Jesus, and Salome went to anoint the body of Jesus with prepared spices. They wondered how they would get into the tomb, but when they arrived the large stone had already been rolled back. In the tomb there was a young man dressed in white. He told them to give a message to the disciples to meet Jesus in Galilee. But the women were afraid, ran from the tomb and said nothing to anyone.

The Empty Tomb – by Matthew (see *Matthew* 28)

Towards dawn on Sunday, Mary Magdalene and the other Mary went to see the tomb of Jesus. As they arrived there was an earthquake and an angel rolled back the stone and sat on it. There were guards at the tomb and they trembled with fear and then became like dead men. The angel told the women not to be afraid, but to tell the disciples to meet Jesus in Galilee. With fear and joy the women went to tell the disciples.

The Empty Tomb – by Luke (see *Luke* 24)

At dawn on Sunday the women who had followed Jesus from Galilee took spices to Jesus' tomb. They found the stone rolled away but no body. In the tomb they met two men in dazzling clothes who reminded them of Jesus' prediction, that he would be crucified but rise again on the third day. Returning from the tomb they reported all this to the disciples.

THINGS TO DO

1   Make two lists: one of similarities and one of differences in the four accounts.

2   Read Matthew's account again. Look deeper. What was he trying to tell people about the meaning behind the empty tomb?

3   How did Matthew get this meaning across?

Behind the Facts – The Resurrection of Jesus

Further investigation of the case of Jesus of Nazareth reveals that many people claimed to have seen him alive after his death on the cross. His disciples, Mary Magdalene, an enemy of the Christians called Saul and, according to one report, 500 people at one time, saw the Risen Jesus.

One reason why Jesus had been executed was that he was considered to be a threat by the authorities of the day. The same fate awaited any other people who followed him. That was why it was amazing that the disciples were prepared to go out preaching that he had been glorified by God so soon after his death.

The disciples themselves do not appear to have been very remarkable men. Most had been ordinary fishermen before they had been attracted to Jesus' cause. They saw hope in his message of the coming kingdom of God and in the miraculous good work he had done with the poor, the sick and the social outcast.

It seems unlikely that they would deliberately lie about seeing Jesus again after his death. Read the reports of Jesus' appearances for yourself in the closing chapters of the gospels.

Again, the accounts vary somewhat, as the first Christians tried to explain a mystery to their hearers. The important thing though was the message. Here is a summary of Simon Peter's first speech to the people of Jerusalem.

'I and my friends are not drunk, we speak soberly and honestly of Jesus of Nazareth – a man who proved by miracles that he had divine authority. You all allowed him to be handed over to sinful men who had him crucified. But this was all part of God's plan. Now God has raised him from death. I and many others are witnesses of this. What is more, he has given me and all my friends the strength to explain this to everyone.

If you want to join us you must give up all your bad old ways and start a new life. Be baptized! God will spare you from the disaster which will fall on this corrupt nation!' (See *Acts* 2)

That day, according to Acts, about 3,000 people were baptized as followers of Jesus.

THINGS TO DO

1 What does it mean, to be 'glorified by God'?

2 Simon Peter put his life at risk by making such statements. Why do you think he was prepared to do this?

3 Look deeper into this mystery. Imagine yourself as one who 'saw' the Risen Jesus. What difference would this make to the way you feel about life?

2
MIND OUT!

Looking Around

We live in a complex world where it is possible to get instant information from all over the world. The problem is: how do we make sense of it? The TV news presents a world containing a strong mixture of tragedy, murder, high finance, politics, industry, sport and so on. Other programmes, newspapers, radio and magazines offer comment on all the latest developments. Some of these reports challenge us to think carefully about the kind of world we want to live in.

'Look around you' the reports seem to say, 'is this how we should live?'

One major tragedy of recent times has been the war in Rwanda, Africa. Two groups fought each other for political power. Each feared and distrusted the other. Stories of massacres were heard, followed by the evidence of bodies floating in the river. Millions fled for their lives. They ended up in overcrowded refugee camps where many died of cholera or starvation. The rest of the world did not seem ready to cope with a tragedy of this proportion. People in

Britain saw the TV images of death and destruction, but felt helpless, like spectators watching a macabre play.

Food, aid, medical supplies and peace-keeping forces came too late for many Rwandans.

People who think such things could not happen again in Europe should not forget the war in former Yugoslavia. Many British tourists holidayed there before fighting began amongst the people. Soon there were accounts of some groups attempting to wipe out their opponents through programmes of mass slaughter or so-called 'ethnic cleansing'. The world was horrified, but again seemed powerless to stop the war.

Amidst such tragedies, however, there are countless acts of courage, kindness and peace-building. Some political negotiators keep trying to bring peace and some individuals make brave rescue attempts.

One such person is Sally Becker from Hove in Sussex. She went to Bosnia (formerly part of Yugoslavia) because she was 'bored at home and wanted to help'. Despite heavy sniper fire and artillery shelling she succeeded in evacuating five critically ill children from the besieged town of Mostar. The children, two of whom had lost an arm, were eventually flown to the West.

THINGS TO DO

1   What are the advantages and disadvantages of getting 'instant news' from all around the world?

2   What general picture of the world is painted by our newspapers? How do you feel about this 'newspaper world'?

Peace in Our Time

According to one Sikh and Hindu way of thinking, we are living at a very bad time in history. It is a time where the truth is forgotten and spiritual practice is mocked. We live in an age of wars and social disintegration. We will need a great deal of faith, determination and help from God if we are to make spiritual progress. This age is known as the Kalyug.

Guru Nanak dramatically described the Kalyug as a 'dark night of falsehood' where 'the moon of truth cannot be seen rising anywhere'. (AG 145)

Since there is no end to the Kalyug in sight, Sikhs must always think and act with God in mind. According to the Sikhs, to say that we can manage without God is a big mistake in this age. Purely human interest will lead to the sorts of disasters we see on the news most days: wars started by pride, materialism and lack of forgiveness; crimes provoked by lust and greed; disputes caused by lack of understanding, generosity and humility.

Sikhs are advised to 'be traders in truth, moderate in eating and sleeping'. (AG 939)

Work, worship and charity should dominate a Sikh's life.

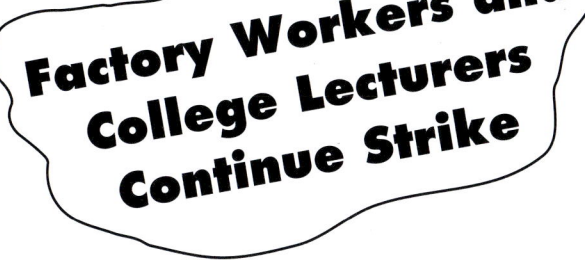

Refugees Flee Rwanda

Terrorists attack helpless villagers

Inheritance row splits family

Factory Workers and College Lecturers Continue Strike

THINGS TO DO

1 Could the world we live in be worse? What things stop it from getting worse?

2 Imagine yourself being involved in one of the headline stories above. Write up your story as if for an inside page of the newspaper.

3 Following the advice to Sikhs on this page, think of ways of bringing peace to each of the newspaper stories.

4 Draw an abstract design entitled 'The Dark Night of Falsehood'.

5 Silently reflect on the idea of 'Traders in Truth'.

Going Against the Grain – Two Prophets

If you suffer a lot in your own life does it help you to understand the suffering in the world? It could just make you angry or bitter. Or it could stir you to action. Many people have used their experience of hardship to help others who may be in the same situation.

HOSEA OF ISRAEL (c.750 BCE)

The Jewish prophet, Hosea, lived in troubled times. Much of the problem, he felt, lay in the fact that the people had got their values badly mixed up. Instead of sticking to the God of Israel they had started worshipping things that had no more power than a piece of wood!

As well as that, they had plotted against and assassinated good men and they were full of lies and deceit. This would surely lead the whole nation to disaster. The story of Hosea tells how he married a prostitute knowing that she would be unfaithful to him. Despite her adultery, Hosea forgave her. Hosea was suffering to show how God suffered when his people followed false gods. Constant love, loyalty and justice were what was required from the people. If they returned to these principles God would save them. Then, God said, 'I will be to the people of Israel like rain in a dry land'. (*Hosea* 14:5)

JOHN THE BAPTIST (c.7 BCE-27 CE)

Another man whose life of hardship reminded people of the really important things in life was John the Baptist. People believed him to be a prophet who had gained spiritual insight from his sparse life in the desert.

John's clothes were made of camel's hair; he wore a leather belt around his waist, and his food was locusts and wild honey. (*Matthew* 3:4)

Christians believe that John prepared the way for Jesus. The kingdom of God was near, he said, so people should get their lives in order.

He had an uncomfortable message for certain groups of people. The religious authorities of the time were amongst those he called snakes. They would not be saved by their religious traditions. People in God's Kingdom would be judged by their good deeds.

'Whoever has two shirts must give one to the man who has none, and whoever has food must share it.' (*Luke* 3:11)

THINGS TO DO

1   Think of a time when you felt angry or irritated. Would Hosea's principles of love, loyalty and justice have helped the situation?

2   Have you ever been generous to people who have less than you? How does your answer make you feel?

The Messenger – Muhammad in Makkah

For Muslims, Muhammad is the last Prophet and Messenger of God. He first received the words of Allah through the angel Jibreel (or Gabriel as the angel is called in the Christian Bible). The words were all memorized and written down, eventually to form the Muslim holy book, the Qur'an.

The experience of receiving God's message was not a painless one. Muhammad described how revelation came to him in different ways.

> 'Sometimes the words strike directly at my heart, like the ringing of a bell, and this is physically hard on me.'

> 'Not once did I receive a revelation without thinking that my soul had been torn away.'

When the Prophet took the words of Allah to the local people in Makkah, he was ridiculed. Some said he was mad. Muhammad spoke out against idol worship and people started to worry that Makkah would lose importance as a resort for pilgrims if his words were taken seriously.

More and more people joined Muhammad and became Muslims (those who submit to the will of God). Amongst the early converts were women, slaves and young men. They had a tough time. Many were tortured for their faith. On at least one occasion, a slave was tied at the ankles then dragged through the streets paved with rough, jagged stones, 'leaving him a lacerated mass of bruises and bleeding cuts'. Muhammad could not do much to prevent such injustice at this point. He advised patience and faith, assuring them that Allah would open a way for them.

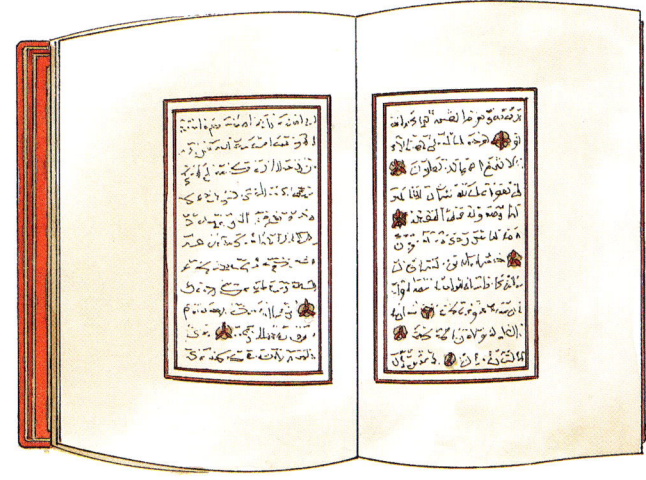

The Glorious Qur'an

Muslims at Prayer (Western China)

THINGS TO DO

1. Why do you think receiving revelation was painful for Muhammad?

2. Imagine you are the slave or know the slave in the story above. Describe how you feel about this incident and write a short prayer to Allah.

3. Think of a time when you could have stood up for what was right, but kept quiet. Describe how you felt then, and how you feel about it now.

3
MIND IN!

Looking Inside

With the world in its apparent state, it is no wonder that many people look inside themselves for peace.

The outside world, the environment, is what is called the **objective** world. It is the world we can examine with our senses, and with technological equipment.

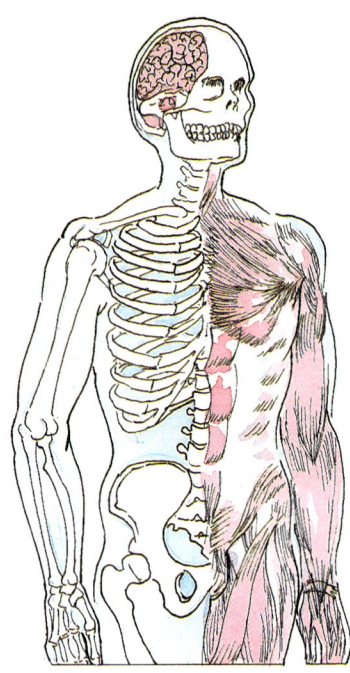

The inner world, our feelings, preferences and so on, is the other side of the coin. It is known as the **subjective** world.

Inside, in the subjective world, we are a seething mass of emotions, daydreams, intentions and so on.

Stop for a moment and think . . . What is to be found inside? Is there a soul, spirit or life-force deep within, making us who we are?

Where is the key to understanding of our own subjective world?

Some say it is in **dreams.** Dreams often make an odd combination of the subjective and objective worlds.

Some psychiatrists use dream interpretation to provide clues about a person's deepest fears and concerns. If these can be sorted out, it is thought, a person can become more calm and together.

Others say the key is in calming the busy mind. **Meditation** can reveal the true self and help a person make spiritual progress.

Others say the key is in **language.** On this theory, the richer your vocabulary and ability to communicate, the richer your world will be, both inside and out!

THINGS TO DO

1 In small groups, say whether you think it is worth trying to interpret dreams or not. Elect a spokesperson to report back to the class on the ideas and examples given by your group.

2 Try a quiet thinking exercise in search of your 'essential nature'.

3 In pairs with one observer, try the 'word association' game for 30 seconds. Let the observer comment on the associations made, then swap roles.

Human Nature – The 'Monster' Within

About a hundred years ago Robert Louis Stevenson wrote a book called, *The Strange Case of Dr Jekyll and Mr Hyde*.

In the story, Dr Jekyll, a respectable man, is worried that he has a weak inner nature. He wants to get rid of his bad side and so works to invent a medicine which will separate his good and evil sides. The mixture works, but it is the evil side, represented by Mr Hyde, who eventually takes over and destroys Dr Jekyll.

In reality, it is not so easy to separate our good and bad nature. The question of what counts as good and what counts as bad is not always so clear either!

In any case, mental health probably involves a realistic acceptance of our whole nature, alongside the ability to take some control over our thoughts and actions.

BUDDHIST MEDITATION

According to Buddhists, meditation has many benefits for the inner life of a person.

Amongst the benefits of meditation are:

CONTENTMENT CONFIDENCE DELIGHT RESPECT GLADNESS LONGER LIFE JOY VIGOUR

Such benefits might not come immediately. Regular and determined practice, and a good teacher or guru will be needed.

Consider the following meditation exercise and, if you feel comfortable with it, try it for yourself:

Place an object such as a cup or pencil in front of you. Sit in a comfortable position, with your back straight and your head up. Direct your attention on your forehead between your eyebrows. Then occupy your mind with the object before you. If your mind starts to wander gently shake off those thoughts as if it were dust on your clothes. Meet thoughts of hatred with compassion. Each time, let those thoughts go their own way and gently return your mind to the object. Don't try too hard! Let your mind move gently. Feel relaxed and content when you finish the meditation. Don't expect immediate results.

THINGS TO DO

1   Cut out a large circle of paper. On one side write all the things you would expect of Dr Jekyll and on the other, Mr Hyde's characteristics.

2   Do we all have a 'monster' inside us? Do we have a good part too? Explain your views.

3   What do you do to stop yourself acting on impulse all the time?

The Peace of God

Moon Hill in China

There is also a long tradition of meditation in Christianity. It can be seen as the listening part of prayer. By calming the selfish needs and concerns, and focusing on God or a prayer or a verse from scripture, Christians may gain new strength for their life.

According to one Christian writer:

'Meditation is the way of making full contact with your own spirit, of making full contact with truth . . . Meditate every morning and every evening, faithfully, simply and humbly. (From *Moment of Christ* John Main OSB)

John Main OSB, who founded the Benedictine Priory of Montreal, recommends the use of a mantra in meditation.

A mantra is a prayer-phrase or prayer-word. One such word is . . .

MARANATHA

This is one of the most ancient Christian prayers. It is an Aramaic word, the language of Jesus. It is a prayer inviting God to bring his kingdom fully into the world. The method is simple:

'When you are seated and still, close your eyes and then begin to repeat, interiorly and silently in your heart, the word Maranatha . . . say it like

this: 'Ma-ra-na-tha'. Four equally stressed syllables. Most people say it in conjunction with their breathing, but that isn't of the essence. The essence requires that you say the word from beginning to end and continue to say it right through your meditation time. The speed should be something that is fairly slow, fairly rhythmical – 'Ma-ra-na-tha'. And that is all you need to know in order to meditate. You have a word, and you say your word, and you remain still. (From *Moment of Christ*)

Eventually, says Main, even the word will disappear and you will be left alone, enlightened and strengthened by the peace of God.

THINGS TO DO

1 What sort of truth can be found through meditation, do you think? Get some ideas from the whole class before you write up your answer.

2 Great care should be taken with choosing a mantra. What do you think might be the result of someone choosing the wrong sort of mantra?

3 Make up a mantra that you think would suit you. What ideas appeal to you?

Anger, Lust and Dishonesty – The Sermon on the Mount

'Drinking and driving', the saying goes, 'wrecks lives'. There are quite a few other things in our society which wreck lives too: murder, arson, blackmail, slander, just for example.

There are strict penalties in law for all of these crimes, yet people continue to commit them. Why?

There are clues to this in a sermon Jesus gave on a hillside.

In this sermon Jesus spoke about right and wrong. There were some things that people did which everyone agreed were wrong, such as murder, adultery and breaking solemn promises. But what about being angry with people, or showing contempt for them because you think you're better than them? Or what about ruining someone's reputation by calling them a worthless fool? Some people do this without a thought. But just like drinking and driving, anger, contempt and slander can wreck lives too.

Everyone agreed, also, that a person involved in a sexual relationship outside their marriage (adultery) was in the wrong and should be punished. Adultery involves dishonesty and dishonesty can lead to family breakdown. But where does it start? Jesus got right to the point:

> 'Anyone who looks at a woman and wants to possess her is guilty of committing adultery with her in his heart.' *(Matthew 5:27)*

Naturally, people will find sexual attraction in others, but it is the 'wanting to possess' that starts the damage. Again, people agreed that it was wrong to break a solemn promise, but some people had been making promises with let-out clauses that allowed them, they thought, to back out later.

Why couldn't they just be straightforward and honest? Jesus said:

> 'Just say "Yes" or "No" – anything else you say comes from the Evil One.' *(Matthew 5:37)*

THINGS TO DO

1 Here are five emotions that people might feel at some points in their life:
ANGER
SEXUAL DESIRE
GREED
FEAR OF GETTING INTO TROUBLE
JEALOUSY
In pairs:
(a) give a definition of each emotion
(b) give an example of the bad things that might happen if each of these emotions gets out of control.

2 Make a class poster warning people of the dangers of each emotion.

4

MIND OVER MATTER

So what exactly is the power of the human mind? Can a mind move solid objects? Can mindpower lift a person from the ground (levitation)? Can one mind really read the thoughts of another (telepathy)? Can a person **think** themselves to recovery from disease or illness?

The human mind does not seem to obey the ordinary laws of physics. It is no respecter of time or space. You can use your mind to recall the past or imagine the future. You can picture yourself in the room next door, or in another country or on a different planet! Where is your mind now?

With practice, your mind could create a whole new world to live in. Does that do any good? Maybe not in the short term, but all improvements in life started off as an idea in someone's mind. The truth is that mind is gaining an increasing hold over matter.

We ourselves may be made of matter, but we use our minds to overcome our physical limitations.

On its own, however, mind itself seems limited. Mind needs to use physical things to achieve its goals.

Technology, in other words, should be about applying our ideas to help us live more comfortable or more fulfilled lives. Think of how technology has been used to help the lives of people who are disabled in some way. Wheelchairs, for example, have been around for a long time, but it is only fairly recently that wheelchairs have been designed to allow the user to play in a number of competitive sports.

Plenty of mind power has been invested in developing new forms of energy to heat, light and run electrical appliances in the home. Which do you think are the best sources of energy?

Computer technology has been used to take drudgery out of some people's jobs. Many tasks on the factory production line are now performed by computer-controlled robots.

In medicine and in communications, laser and optical fibre technology appear to have benefits that will continue to improve the quality of human life well into the future.

THINGS TO DO

1   There are lots of questions on this page. In twos and threes discuss your feelings on each question. Do you all agree? What **other** views might there be?

2   Think of some examples where technology has **not** helped towards more fulfilled lives. What went wrong would you say?

3   Are you basically optimistic or pessimistic about human use of technology?

Zacchaeus – Learning to Live in the Present

There is often a clash in life between the dictates of the heart and those of the mind. This story may help you to sort out some of the issues.

Zacchaeus was a traitor to his own people. He collected taxes for the Romans, who had taken control of his country, Judaea.

He was rich, but not happy. People did not like Zacchaeus, but they dared not harm him. He was a little man, but he was protected by the Romans.

To everyone's surprise, Jesus spoke to Zacchaeus. What's more, he said he'd like to eat at Zaccheaus' house. This was seen as a great honour for Zacchaeus.

Zacchaeus got it right. He promised to give half his wealth to the poor, and to pay back anyone he had cheated. No more trying to forget his past. No more illusions about the future. Zacchaeus was going to live in the present. He had cleared his conscience and that, said Jesus, was salvation.

He had no friends so he just took as much as he could. But when Jesus visited his town, Jericho, something told him he should be there.

Zacchaeus felt bad about the past and knew that money would not bring an end to his unhappiness. He climbed a tree to see Jesus when the crowd would not let him near.

THINGS TO DO

1 Why was Zacchaeus disliked? Write down as many reasons as you can.

2 Jesus doesn't seem to do much in this story. Why do you think he had such a deep effect on Zacchaeus?

Dealing with Guilt – The Story of Angulimala

At the time of the Buddha there lived a young man called Ahimsaka. He was a good student, hard-working and intelligent. Others became jealous of him and soon he became an outcast, rejected by his friends, teachers and even his family. No one would employ him, so he turned to a life of crime.

He became a highway robber, often killing his victims, and cutting off their little fingers. He made a necklace of these fingers and wore them around his neck. He became known as Angulimala, meaning 'necklace of little fingers'. Angulimala terrorized people for years, killing even those who pleaded for mercy, until one day he met a monk.

Angulimala was amazed at the monk's calm and peaceful manner. Why was he not afraid? Why did he show no hatred towards him? Angulimala collapsed at the feet of the monk. From that day, he never again killed a living being.

The monk turned out to be the Buddha himself, and Angulimala decided that he, too, would become a monk and follow the Buddha. In fact, he became one of the Buddha's greatest followers, giving help to the sick and the poor.

One day, however, Angulimala met the son of one of his victims. He was full of guilt as he remembered all the other people's lives he had ruined during his time as a murderous robber. He sank into a deep depression and wondered what he could do. He felt guilty and thought that he had no future. The situation seemed hopeless.

Angulimala's depression was noticed by the Buddha. With soothing words, the Buddha encouraged the ex-murderer to go on with his search for inner peace.

Angulimala made up for his past deeds by helping to save the life of a pregnant woman. At last he had true peace of mind. But not everyone recognized the change that had taken place.

Some villagers thought that he had disguised himself as a monk in order to kill more people and chop off more fingers for his gruesome collection. As he walked around the village Angulimala was attacked and savagely beaten. He was left to die like a dog.

But Angulimala was not dead. In great pain he stumbled back to the Buddha's monastery. Throughout the attack Angulimala had remained calm. He felt no bitterness towards his attackers. He had conquered his guilt, his cruelty and his anger. At this point, he died.

Buddhists believe that Angulimala had attained Nirvana, where there is no suffering whatsoever.

THINGS TO DO

1 Outline the factors which led Ahimsaka into a life of crime.

2 Why do you think Ahimsaka chopped off the little fingers of his victims?

3 What do you think Angulimala was **feeling** when he collapsed at the Buddha's feet?

4 How did the Buddha's words help Angulimala come to terms with his guilt?

5 What do you think Angulimala was thinking and feeling while he was being beaten up?

6 'Angulimala wasted his life.' Do you agree?

5

FEEL THE FORCE

Out of Control

Are you in control of your life? Or is life in control of you? You probably feel at times that you are pushed around. Sometimes it is other people who tell us what to do or not to do. But sometimes things happen that, it seems, **no one** can do anything about.

People's lives can be ended or completely changed by lightning, earthquakes, plagues, storms and floods; things which insurance companies used to call 'acts of God' because no one else could be held responsible!

In January 1995 for example, thousands of people were killed when an earthquake hit the town of Kobe in Japan.

In 1978, Morecambe in Lancashire was declared a National Disaster Area when storms swept away the west pier, took roofs off many houses and brought the sea crashing through shops and houses along the promenade. Many people faced financial ruin.

The worst natural disaster of modern times is probably the circular storm of 1970 which accounted for about a million lives on the Ganges Delta Islands.

In Britain most people over 35 years old will remember the Aberfan disaster. 144 people, mostly children, died when a coal tip landslide engulfed a school in South Wales. It was a tragedy which shocked the nation. No doubt human miscalculation was partly to blame, though few could have guessed the tragic consequences.

Some individuals seem to be particularly unlucky when it comes to nature. Roy C Sullivan of Virginia, USA, was struck by lightning **seven** times. On two occasions his hair was set on fire. Is anyone to blame for such events?

A lot of suffering is caused by greed, selfishness and prejudice, but what about these disasters? There cannot be a God, some people say, because if God is good, such things would not happen! But could God have a purpose that outweighs all this suffering? Even if religions offer no certain answers to these questions, it is sure that where such disasters occur you will find many religious people bringing support and comfort to those who are suffering.

THINGS TO DO

1   Split into pairs. One person should argue that all disasters are avoidable. The other that often, no one is to blame.

2   Sometimes people make so-called sick jokes about disasters. Why do you think they do this? How do you think relatives of disaster victims feel about these 'jokes'?

3   Reflect silently for a while and imagine that there is some great purpose to all the suffering in the world. Picture it in shapes, colours, textures, movement. Draw and colour the result. Explain the symbolism in your drawing.

Accidents Will Happen

'A carriage without horse shall go
Disaster fill the world with woe.'
(The Prophecies of Mother Shipton
[1488-1561])

The forces and power of the universe are vast and hard to imagine, but human beings have now taken hold of some of those forces. We are quickly discovering that this new-found power can be helpful or harmful, depending on how it is used. Nuclear energy, for instance, might provide us with the electricity we need to keep our present lifestyle going, but what will be the ultimate cost? Will nuclear waste be safely stored? Will the technology that creates nuclear power be used in the end to make weapons that might destroy the whole world? There are already enough nuclear weapons in existence to wipe out life on earth several times over.

Another example of human manipulation of natural forces is the invention of the motor car. As Heathcote Williams says in his poem about cars, *Autogeddon*, more than 17 million people have been killed in road traffic accidents in the hundred years since Karl Benz constructed the first automobile.

Williams imagined what an alien visitor to this planet might think, observing the world domination of the motor car. Cars are a kind of god, it would seem, demanding a constant stream of human sacrifices to keep them going. The visitor might wonder if human blood was needed to keep the roads lubricated for motor travel.

On an average day, in Britain alone, 10 people will be killed on the road and many more will be seriously injured. In a whole year the victims of road traffic accidents far outweigh those of, say, aeroplane disasters. Yet we seem complacent. We consider car travel to be an acceptable risk. We see the benefits of technology but prefer not to look too closely at the dangers.

THINGS TO DO

1   How does the information on this page make you feel?

2   Make two lists; one of the benefits of cars, and one of the dangers.

3   Imagine you are the 'alien visitor' of Heathcote Williams' poem. Write down your thoughts as you observe four teenagers stealing a car for a joyride.

4   Are human beings now obtaining godlike powers? What responsibilities go with such powers?

Destroyer and Saviour

You may already be familiar with the Hindu aspect of God called Shiva. Shiva, seen here dancing on the demon of ignorance, is sometimes called the Destroyer of universes. This is not the whole story, however, for Shiva is also the Creator. In fact, Shiva has a role to play in explaining all the powers and energies in the universe. As Shiva Nataraja, he is 'Lord of the dance'. When he dances wildly, the whole world shakes.

Shiva can also spare the world from disaster. In his hair is a symbol of the River Ganges, which would have flooded the earth if he had not caught it in his hair when it first came down from the heavens. His throat is usually coloured blue because when the great oceans were churning a poison was created that would have destroyed the world. Shiva alone was strong enough to swallow the poison and save the world.

For many Hindus, Shiva is the great cosmic power, linking good and evil, ever changing, ever creating, destroying and creating again.

Look at other symbols in the picture including:

- the drum – the rhythm of the dance of creation

- the serpent (cobra) – poison/healing/cosmic energy

- the ring of fire – the life process of the universe

- the raised right hand – 'Do not fear'

- hand pointing to foot – 'Take refuge'.

THINGS TO DO

1   The 'dance of life' includes both birth and death. Reflect silently on the idea of the dance of life. What colours, shapes, sounds, movements, spring to mind?

2   Sketch out your ideas for a poster on 'the dance of life'.

LEVELS OF MEANING

As with all Hindu mythology the stories and symbols can be understood at different levels. At one level, these ideas can be seen as an entertaining explanation of the way everything is changing in the universe.

At another level, the Hindu believer might be reminded that all of their own words and actions will produce reverberations, like the beating of Shiva Nataraja's drum.

Take Power!

We may not yet be able to control the weather, or avoid all mechanical accidents, but human beings are gaining more and more power and control in the world. Genetic engineering, for example, may give us the power to redirect even the forces of evolution.

Christians will have something to say about the way such power should be used.

Jesus himself seemed to possess many powers and he had to decide how to use them. Jesus did not try to give everybody what they wanted. He was not interested in impressing people with meaningless stunts. He did not try to gain political power. This was not his main mission. He rejected these paths at his temptation in the Judaean desert. But using his remarkable powers was not out of the question. There are stories about Jesus miraculously feeding hungry people, stilling a storm when his disciples feared for their lives and bravely going into Jerusalem to turn out the money-changers who were misusing the temple, knowing he could be arrested and executed for such an act. We may not be capable of such acts of compassion and bravery but perhaps

we can do something in this modern world to change people's lives for the better.

If anyone wanted power, said Jesus, they should be like the Son of Man, 'who did not come to be served, but to serve and to give his life to redeem many people'. (*Matthew* 20:28)

THINGS TO DO

1   Draw three more cartoons, showing how good people today are trying to:
    (a) help the poor and starving,
    (b) use medical technology to save or improve life and,
    (c) use political or military action to save or protect people.

2   How could a person gain more power and authority by being a servant?

6
SEEING IS BELIEVING

So far we've been looking at the objective world, the subjective world and the way Christianity and other religions help us make sense of it all.

But how are we to test these views for ourselves? In the second half of this book we'll be considering the evidence of our eyes, our ears, our exploration of the world and the experience of believers.

Illusions and Magic

Some people, quite wisely perhaps, will not believe anything unless they see it for themselves. What happens, though, when you can't trust what you see?

What do you see here; two faces or a vase? You may have seen this sort of picture before, but have you realized the point?

The point is, everything that we see is **interpreted** by us. We look for things that we recognize and this is why we are so easy to fool. Magicians on the TV know that the hand can move quicker than the eye and are able to create illusions that seem impossible.

Try this illusion based on the way our eyes deal with colour. Look at the union flag for about a minute. Then look at the blank space below for a while until the flag appears in its correct colours.

If this works for you it is because the optical nerves tend to produce the complementary colours of the light spectrum. Things we take for granted are not all that they seem to be!

Think of a person going across the desert with no water. Suddenly an oasis appears ahead, but then it disappears. It was a mirage!

THINGS TO DO

1 Describe to the person next to you an illusion or magic trick you have seen or heard of. Do you know how the trick is done or why the brain is fooled?

2 What do these illusions make you feel about the world around you?

3 Write a dialogue between two people, one who thinks the world is a better place than it 'really' is, and one who thinks it's worse. Remember, **you** may be one of the characters!

Picture This

Pictures, statues and images are very important in Hinduism. They often symbolize characteristics of the nature of God, or of the Created Universe.

They can be used in a number of ways, according to a person's own spiritual development and need.

Pictured here is Ganesha. He is the son of Shiva (see p27) and Parvati. Any act of worship or new enterprise may begin with worship of Ganesha as he is the focus for overcoming obstacles.

His body is large and he is a bit clumsy. Hindus say this reflects the fact that inner beauty and perfection have little to do with outward appearance.

His elephant head shows great intelligence, symbolizing the need to use one's brain in new enterprises.

A snare or noose is held in one hand, reminding the worshipper that material possessions and attachments are a trap. In another hand a weapon will prod the believer into the right moral path.

Another hand holds a dish of sweets (**modala**), as a reminder of how sweet the inner self is. The fourth hand is open in a sign of blessing.

At his feet is a mouse. For some, the mouse symbolizes the obstacles to be overcome. For others it is a reminder of the importance of all creatures, whatever their size.

THE MAHABHARATA

Ganesha has an important role to play in Hindu scriptures. He is believed to have written down the world's longest poem, the Mahabharata. His broken tusk which you see in the picture, was used to write down the poem, as dictated to him by the Sage Vyasa.

The main story of the poem is about a war between two branches of a family, but contains many stories within the main story.

All this from one picture, and more besides!

THINGS TO DO

1   What were your first thoughts and feelings about the picture of Ganesha?

2   What do you think now, having read about the symbolism in the picture?

3   Find pictures of other Hindu gods. Perhaps you can guess at some of the symbolism by looking carefully and reflecting on the meaning of the picture or statue.

See for Yourself – Testing the Truth . . .

IN BUDDHISM

At the time of the Buddha, as now, there were many groups of people who claimed they had the truth about life and the right way to live.

Knowing the Buddha to be the wisest of teachers, some rulers of a town approached him with a question.

> 'There are hermits and priests,' they said, 'who come to this town recommending their view of life and showing contempt for all other views. Then there are other hermits and priests who come and do the same. How can we tell who is telling the truth and who is telling lies?

The Buddha said they were right to worry, because such views were open to doubt.

He told them:

> 'Don't go by hearsay or by tradition, nor out of respect to hermits or priests, nor even by argument or inference or reflection on opinion.

> But when you know yourself that the teachings are not good and are condemned by the wise because, when put into practice, they lead to loss and suffering, then reject them.'
> (Ang. Nik. i. 188)

IN ISLAM

For Muslims the truth cannot be known by human thinking alone. What is needed is the help of Allah. Allah's words for the guidance of all humankind are in the Holy Qur'an. After that we are left to our own free choice. We are invited to meditate on the words of the Qur'an and accept its teaching if we are gifted with understanding. (38:29)

In the name of Allah, most gracious, most merciful.

بِسْمِ اللَّهِ الرَّحْمَنِ الرَّحِيمُ

Allah himself reveals the Truth to those who desire to follow him. Allah

leads them out of every kind of darkness into the light by His Will, and guides them along the right path. (5:16-17)

Human teachers are influenced and guided by others, but only Allah can teach the pure Truth. (10:35)

How can this be tested? Only by following the will of Allah in leading a moral life. The purer a person's life, the greater their grasp of the Truth. (56:78-80)

THINGS TO DO

1 Have a class discussion about untrue things you believed when you were a child. How did you feel when you found out the truth?

2 Some people try to rely on their feelings to guide them towards truth. What do you think
   (a) Buddhists and
   (b) Muslims might say about this?

It's a Miracle – Christian Healing

In Christianity, as in Islam and Judaism, there are two main ways in which truth is known. One is through observation of and reflection on the beauty of nature because it is seen as evidence of God's existence and purpose.

The other way of knowing Truth is through God's **revelation.** The Holy Scriptures are held to be an example of God's Word being revealed to people. Another example of God's revelation is to be seen in the help Christians give to those who are suffering in some way.

MELVIN BANKS

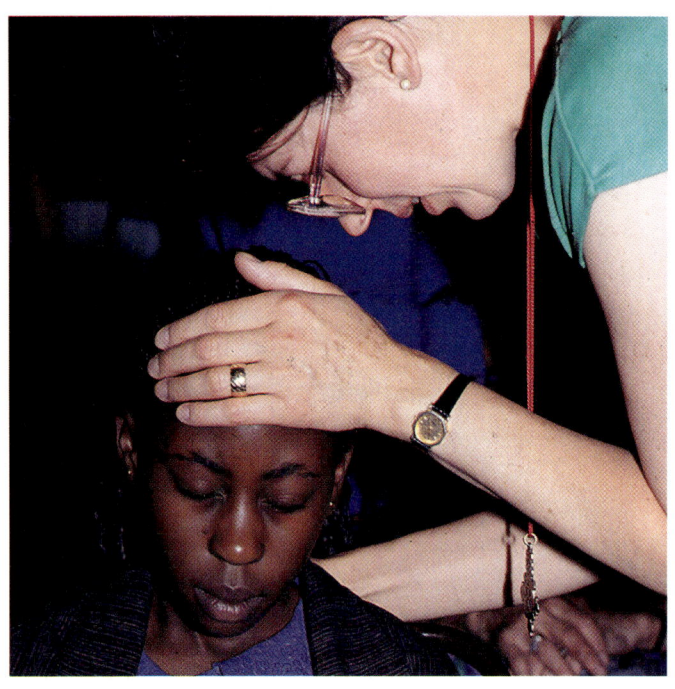

Christian Healing

Rev. Melvin Banks believes that God has worked through him to bring healing to many people. Sometimes his prayers for people who are ill help them to feel better, without curing the physical illness. But on many occasions the results of prayer have been, he claims, truly miraculous.

A woman with arthritis came to him. The doctor had told her she would never be able to unclench her fists because of the arthritis. Melvin Banks put his hands on hers and prayed. When he opened his eyes he was astonished. The woman was crying and her fingers were slowly unfolding. She flexed them and rubbed her hands together. Melvin too began to weep, thankful, he says, to God for answering his prayer. The woman was never troubled by arthritis again, and even joined the church sewing group!

Of course, not everyone is healed in this way. One lady who came for healing threw down her crutches in the belief that she had been healed of the arthritis in her knee joints. Sadly, she was wrong and had to return to hospital, having lost all hope of recovery.

BISHOP MORRIS MADDOCKS

Christians are not only interested in faith healing. Many Christians are involved in all sorts of areas of health care; physical, mental and spiritual.

Bishop Morris Maddocks believes that the Christian has been sent out 'among the sick and the poor, the underprivileged and the hungry, the anxiety-ridden and the downtrodden, to proclaim the fact that Christ heals and saves.' (From *The Christian Healing Ministry*)

It doesn't take a miracle to give love and care to such people, or to stand up for them when they are down. Many Christians do voluntary or professional work to help those whom society seems to devalue. When people do this, says the Bishop, they are not far from the Kingdom of God.

THINGS TO DO

1   What is a 'healthy' person?

2   Think of a time when you were ill or in pain. What things helped you get better?

7

LISTEN

Can You Hear Me?

This is the information age. It's possible now via computer technology to find out everything about anything. Well, almost! But in the middle of this information bombardment have we forgotten who we are? For some people it seems important to find their identity in the traditions and culture of their ancestors.

ROOTS

Alex Haley

One such person is Alex Haley, a black American, who wrote a book called *Roots*, about seven generations of his ancestors. Most of his information came from stories told by his grandmother and elderly relatives. He finally traced his ancestry back to an African called Kin-tay who had been taken to America as a slave. Kin-tay was from the Gambia. Alex went to the Gambia and, according to the book, found an old man who had been trained to remember the centuries-old histories of villages, of clans, of families, of great heroes. There was no writing in these villages and the old man was, in turn, teaching some selected pupils to learn the histories off by heart. This is what happened when

Alex met him: 'The old man sat down, facing me as the people hurriedly gathered behind him. Then he began to recite for me the ancestral history of the Kin-tay (Kinte) clan, as it had been passed down orally across the centuries from the forefathers' time. . . . It was all just unbelievable!'

After two hours the old man reached a detail in the narrative that Alex recognised, as translated by the interpreter – 'About the time the King's soldiers came, the eldest of these four sons went away from his village to chop wood and he was never seen again.'

'I sat as if I were carved of stone. This man whose lifetime had been in this back-country African village had no way in the world to know that he had just echoed what I had heard all through my boyhood years on my grandma's front porch . . . of an African who had always insisted that his name was 'Kin-tay'; . . . and who had been kidnapped into slavery while not far from his village, chopping wood, to make himself a drum.'

Alex was later able to track down a written record of the actual slaveship that had brought his ancestor to America on 20 September 1767!

THINGS TO DO

1   Write a story of something about yourself or your family that you would like future generations to remember.

2   Suppose you were listening to stories about your ancestors and you discovered that one of them had been enslaved by traders. How would you feel about that? How important is it to know something about your family history?

The Dark Face of Reality

We may or may not be able to hear about our ancestral history. Perhaps it is more important anyway, to listen to what is going on around us. Spiritual writer, Martin Israel, assesses the present situation like this:

> We are moving to the close of a century torn apart with organized violence of such ferocity that those of us who have witnessed some of the drama of our time and are still alive, miraculously preserved in body and mind, quake inwardly at the sheer horror of it all.
> (From *The Dark Face of Reality*)

It is getting more and more difficult to understand our own place in the scheme of things in the middle of all the noise and bustle in the modern world.

Think about your day. Do you listen to the radio, watch TV in the morning? Is your family noisy or argumentative? Is there much traffic on your way to school? What sort of noises irritate you at school; other pupils, teachers, bells going every five minutes?

Many people feel the need to get away from all the noise of the modern world to sort themselves out and come to terms with the different 'voices' pushing them this way and that. They may go on 'retreat', a place where they can find some peace, and listen to their own thoughts and feelings for a change. This practice of constructive listening is called **contemplation** and sometimes involves prayer. It can sometimes be an uncomfortable experience, because deep contemplation can help a person see themselves as they really are, with all their faults and weaknesses.

A Buddhist monk

THINGS TO DO

1   Just stay quiet for a few minutes and listen. Focus your attention on noises inside the classroom, then just outside, then further into the distance.

2   Write a short story or poem about noise.

3   With the help of your teacher try an awareness exercise to become more aware of your own physical and mental make-up.

Talk is Life

Listening to what is going on around us is important, but what are we doing with the words we hear? Words are the very stuff of human life. Words can hurt. Words can deceive and betray. But words can also create, build, encourage and give hope.

Sometimes words are written down and given special significance by certain groups of people. The words in the Qur'an or the Bible, for example, are believed by millions of people to be the Words of God. These words were given to chosen individuals who were 'inspired' to transmit them, usually for others to write down. Believers consider these words to be of vital importance because they come from the One who created everything by use of commands, (See *Qur'an* 2:117 or *Genesis* 1). When written down these words become 'scriptures' and must be treated with respect.

LISTEN AND LEARN

The ability to listen with care and sensitivity has played an important part in the Sikh religion, too.

Guru Nanak was the first in a line of ten Sikh gurus (religious teachers) who received the word of God. Nanak had an experience of enlightenment when he was 30 years old. He found himself 'in the court of God' where he was given the task of bringing people out of their ignorance into enlightenment. He was able to do this in extraordinary ways.

On one occasion Guru Nanak and a musician friend called Mardana stayed at the house of a wealthy man named Sajjan. The local people thought that Sajjan was a religious man who welcomed strangers with great hospitality. He seemed to spend most of the day in prayer. In fact, however, Sajjan was a murderer. His plan was to invite travellers to his home, then kill them and steal their possessions.

That night, Sajjan waited for Guru Nanak and Mardana to go to sleep. Instead, he heard them playing music, and singing praises to God. As Sajjan listened his mind completely changed. He burst into the room; but instead of killing his guests he fell at Guru Nanak's feet, confessing his crimes and pleading for help.

That day, after hearing the words of God and the music played in his praise, Sajjan gave all his riches to the poor, converted his house into a place to worship God (Gurdwara) and started to pray with real conviction.

THINGS TO DO

1 Words can be used to get things organised. Write down a list of requests or commands that you have heard your teachers use today.

2 When people ask you to do these things, how do you feel? Does it depend on who is asking?

3 (a) What was it about Guru Nanak and Mardana that changed Sajjan?
   (b) Draw a cartoon sequence showing the main events of the story.

4 Reflect silently for a few minutes on a time when you were hurt or angered by words. Remember how you responded, without judging yourself as right or wrong. Then let it all fade into the past. (Make up a situation if you can't think of one.)

Have I Got News For You!

There are other stories of people hearing God's voice. What about Mary, the mother of Jesus for example? According to the gospel of Luke, God sent the angel Gabriel to Mary with this message: 'Don't be afraid, Mary; God has been gracious to you. You will become pregnant and give birth to a son, and you will name him Jesus. He will be great and will be called the Son of the Most High God.'

Mary replied, 'I am a virgin. How, then, can this be?' The angel answered, 'The Holy Spirit will come upon you, and God's power will rest upon you. For this reason the holy child will be called the Son of God.' Mary immediately accepted the news. 'I am the Lord's servant,' she said, 'May it happen to me as you have said.' (*Luke 1:30-38*)

The Annunciation, *by Sandro Botticelli*

When Mary's fiancé, Joseph, learned that she was pregnant, he made plans to break the engagement privately. But, according to Matthew's gospel, an angel appeared to him in a dream and told him not to be afraid to marry her. (*Matthew 1:18-25*)

Now, you might believe that this story is literally true. You might say, if God is all-powerful why couldn't he send such messages and make Mary pregnant in a miraculous way?

Or you might believe that the story was used by the early Christians to show that Jesus was special, and to back up their claim that he was the Saviour foretold by the prophets.

But perhaps both points of view are missing something. Don't forget that we can always learn something from a good story, whether it's true or not!

THINGS TO DO

1   What do you think it feels like to believe you have been chosen by God for a special purpose? How would Mary and Joseph have felt?

2   (a) Reflect silently for a few minutes and imagine you receive a message about one of the problems in the world.
    (b) Write a Haiku poem based on the meditation entitled *The Voice*.

8
BEYOND THE BLACK STUMP

The Black Stump

The Devil's Marbles, Australia

In Australia there was a place beyond which it was foolish for any European settler to travel. It was known as the black stump. It was a sign that living things had come to an end, beyond was only rock and desert. The strange thing was that the European settlers were not altogether right. There was life beyond the black stump, though not the sort of life that the settlers could easily understand.

Many of the rock formations of central Australia are sacred sites for aboriginal peoples. The Aborigines, it is reckoned, had lived in Australia for around 40,000 years, so it was not really correct to think that the place was discovered by Captain Cook in 1770.

The Australian outback was a dangerous place for people who didn't know how to live there. Even now, the European Australians are struggling to understand and value the Aborigine people whose land had been taken by the first settlers. By going out, 'beyond the black stump', by meetings between white and black skinned people, progress is being made and more respect shown for the ancient peoples of Australia and for their beliefs and ways.

Who has more to learn?

THINGS TO DO

1   Write a few paragraphs about a European settler, lost beyond the black stump, not sure of the way back to safety.

2   Study the examples of aboriginal art. Using dots, circles, curved and short lines, earth colours, and a bird's eye view, draw a representation of a creature or plant found in Britain.

Aborigine art at Uluru (Ayer's Rock)

Making Up the Future

'Going forward means taking new risks.'

Do you ever wish you could see into the future? Countless books, films and TV programmes have been based on the idea of human beings travelling into the future and seeing what is in store. Most of these stories are a kind of warning. The writers are telling us to take care if we don't want this or that to happen in the future.

In *Terminator 2*, there is a scientist whose work will lead to the creation of machines which will attempt to destroy all human beings. Sarah Connor, who knows what the future will bring, decides to kill the scientist. At first, she fails, but then she sees him face to face. She has the gun, he is helpless. Killing this man will probably prevent an awful future. What does she do?

We use our imagination to explore the future. What sort of world do we want to live in? What sort of society? What actions will produce the best results?

Films like *Terminator 1* and *2* show the state as a machine and a future world where machines take over. The film asks: 'Is technology going to serve us, or crush us?'

Indirectly we are also being challenged to think about what sort of actions count as good and what count as evil.

THINGS TO DO

1 What would you do in Sarah Connor's position? Explain your actions to the scientist's family.

2 Hot seat. One person sits in the middle of the class, others move around them. This is a visitor from the future. Ask them questions about their way of life. Other 'visitors' then join in.

3 Write an article for the paper about the visitors from the future, based on the Hot Seat role play.

4 Discuss the idea that 'people should always trust their feelings.'

Help from Above

In approximately 1250 BCE, when Moses led the Hebrew people out of slavery in Egypt, no one knew where they were going. They only knew that they were aiming for a 'Promised Land'. Moses told them that this land was a place where God wanted them to be: a land 'flowing with milk and honey'. It was to take them 40 years before they settled there. The journey through the wilderness is described in the book of *Exodus* in the Bible. The story reveals that without the help of God and the faith of Moses, the Hebrews would never have survived.

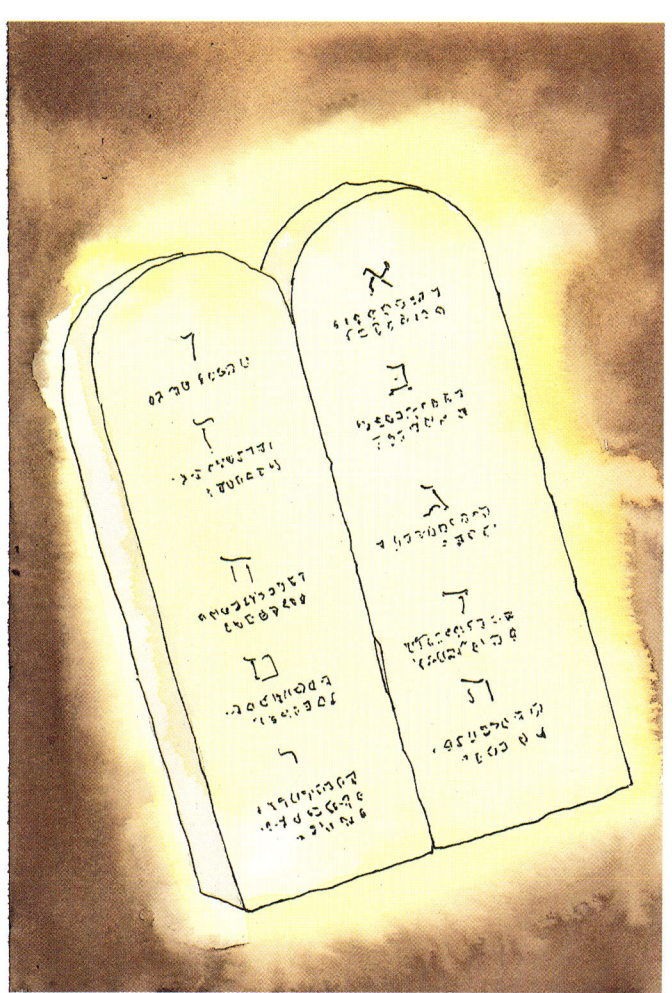

The Parting of the Red Sea by Arthur Szyk

Only three days after their miraculous escape from the Egyptian army, the Hebrews were in trouble. The only water they could find was undrinkable. Moses prayed for help. After his prayer Moses found a piece of wood. When he threw it into the water it became fit to drink.

Six weeks later they were in another desert, with no food. This time a large flock of birds called quails landed on the Hebrew camp, providing plenty to eat.

Following Moses's prayers they found white flakes of food every morning in the desert. They called the food 'manna', meaning 'what is it?'

The Hebrews then found themselves under attack from a tribe called the Amelekites. Again, with God's help, they believed, the Hebrews triumphed.

In exchange for his help, God asked that the Hebrews keep his laws. These laws were the Ten Commandments, which Moses received on Mount Sinai.

THINGS TO DO

1 Do a brainstorm on what kept the Hebrews together while they were in the wilderness.

2 Look deeper into this story. What meaningful answers to questions about life are being offered here?

The Way of Christ

Icon of Christ (14th Century CE)

Christians believe that they are helped in giving their lives to others by the Holy Spirit. This, says Jesus, is the Spirit who reveals the truth about God. The disciples will know this Spirit 'because he remains with you and is in you'. (*John* 14:17)

The disciples claimed that Jesus was the Christ. That is, he was the Messiah or Chosen Saviour, who had been expected by the Jewish people to bring in a new age of God's rule on earth. Clearly things did not work out exactly as most Jews had hoped. Within 40 years of Jesus's death, Jerusalem, the Holy City, had been completely destroyed and the Jewish people once again scattered across the world.

So, either:

- Jesus was NOT the Christ;

- or God's Kingdom had begun with Jesus and would come in fullness at a later date;

- or the Kingdom of God belongs to the life after death;

- or the Kingdom of God is something inside the individual believer;

- or perhaps a combination of two or more parts of these ideas.

Becoming a follower of Jesus is also a journey into the unknown. Many Christians believe that their destination is assured: a place with God; but what happens on the way is less certain.

Jesus himself said that following him would not be easy. He expected there to be divisions in families. He had not brought instant peace with him either. Anyone wishing to be a disciple of Jesus had to take up their cross and follow in his steps. That meant being prepared to give up everything.

THINGS TO DO

1 Christians are commanded to love God and to love their neighbour as themselves. Role play a scene where this might cause family conflict.

2 Recall the 'Maranatha' prayer from chapter 3. Why did the early Christians use this prayer?

3 Make a large 'maranatha' collage using old magazines, cloth and so on. Around the word itself put symbols of your idea of a Kingdom of God.

9
GET IN TOUCH

ECOS *The European Community of Stones*

'No man is an island, entire of himself.' John Donne (1573-1631), who wrote these words, meant that no one in our world can live a completely independent life. There are times when we want to be alone, perhaps, but most of us like to have friends and to be part of something.

Many of the things we most enjoy involve getting together with other people; playing games and sport, going to parties, playing music, going on trips or just hanging out.

Sometimes a lot of organization is involved in making a group work or an event happen. Sometimes people fall out or can't get on with others in the group. All this needs working out if everyone is to get the most out of the group. Communities, and even nations, work a bit like this.

It's been a debate for hundreds of years whether Britain should be part of a European Community of Nations. On the one hand there is a lot to be gained from co-operating with our nearest neighbours. On the other hand, some say, we may lose our independence and right to make our own decisions.

One town in England, Frome, in Somerset, decided to show how co-operation with other countries could forge new friendships, build a lasting memorial and provide the town with an additional facility at the same time.

With the help of a local firm, the town made contact with quarrying companies in each of the member countries of the European Union and persuaded them to send a large stone to represent their country.

The stones form a semi-circle around an open-air amphitheatre. It's a modern 'Stonehenge' within which concerts and entertainments of various sorts go on. More than that, it is a European 'community of stones' (ECOS) which symbolizes the common purposes of industrious, generous and friendly people throughout Europe.

THINGS TO DO

1   In what sense is ECOS a religious building, do you think?

2   Perform a hot seat role play where European visitors of your own age visit your school. One visitor has a very positive view of Britain, another is not so complimentary. Explore the reactions of the group.

3   Design your own symbol of international co-operation.

4   Write a list of words that describe the good things about being in a club/society/gang.

Lay Membership of a Religion – Taking the Plunge

Joining a religious group is much the same as joining another group. It can be a bit scary at first being the new person around. But if the regular members are friendly and if you already know someone who belongs, it's not so bad.

In some religious traditions it is even easier, particularly if you're doing what everyone in the community does. For many, belonging to a religion is a family and community affair. For others it's a completely new venture. Whatever the case, it takes a lot of thought and commitment to decide to follow a system of religious belief.

Anyone who is a member of a religious tradition, but is not ordained (as a priest, monk, nun or official for example), is called a lay person of that religion.

Joining a religious group usually involves some sort of **ritual**. This is a way of publicly marking a new start in a person's life.

In Christianity, the ritual is **baptism**. A person already baptized as a Christian when they were a baby may have a **confirmation** service when they are older.

I WANTED TO BE CONFIRMED TO SHOW THAT I HAVE CHOSEN TO BE A CHRISTIAN MYSELF, NOT JUST BECAUSE MY PARENTS HAD ME CHRISTENED.

JANET, A LAY MEMBER OF THE CHURCH OF ENGLAND

BEING BAPTISED IS FOLLOWING THE EXAMPLE OF JESUS HIMSELF, WHO WAS BAPTISED IN THE RIVER JORDAN. WE ARE ALSO BAPTISED IN THE SPIRIT.

WINNIE, A MEMBER OF THE PENTECOSTAL CHURCH

I WENT IN FOR THE FULL IMMERSION BAPTISM- RIGHT UNDER THE WATER - TO SHOW THAT I'VE GIVEN MYSELF TO CHRIST. THE WATER SYMBOLISES THE WASHING AWAY OF SINS AND STARTING A NEW LIFE

DAVE, A BAPTIST CHRISTIAN

THINGS TO DO

1   What is your most valuable possession? Suppose it was lost or stolen.
    (a) Describe your feelings.
    (b) Describe your life without this possession.

2   What might be courageous about joining a religious group?

3   What difference do you think baptism or confirmation will make to the lives of Janet, David and Winnie?

Contrary to popular opinion, believing is not simply a refuge for the weak or lonely. Calling yourself a Christian, Muslim, Hindu, Buddhist, Jew, Sikh or whatever often involves quite a lot of courage.

Converting to Judaism

It is not at all easy to become a Jew. It is more straightforward if one is **born** Jewish. That is, essentially, one must have a Jewish mother.

Deirdre Burke

Deirdre Burke, from Walsall in the West Midlands, became a Jew in the Progressive tradition of Judaism.

She had been brought up in the Christian faith, but she had not been stirred by the teachings and practices of Christianity.

She first became interested in Judaism when she took Religious Studies 'A' level at school. She wanted to learn more and so chose to study Judaism as part of her university course. During this time she felt a growing emotional attachment to the Jewish people and began to attend worship at the Reform Synagogue in Manchester.

In order to become Jewish, Deirdre had to attend a series of classes and write essays about Judaism and about her reasons for joining the Jewish Community.

Rabbi Julia Neuberger

Then she was interviewed by a panel of Jewish leaders and teachers (rabbis). Finally she attended an induction service, where she recited parts of a Jewish prayer called the Shema and was called up for a blessing.

Deirdre received her certificate and was properly admitted to the Jewish faith.

Here are some sayings that mean a lot to Deirdre:

> Hear, O Israel, the Lord your God is One God, And you shall love the Lord Your God with all your heart, and all your soul, and with all your might.
> ('The Shema' – *Deuteronomy* 6)

> 'If I am not for myself, who will be? But if I am only for myself, what am I? If not now, when?'
> (Hillel – 1st century CE)

> Help us, O Lord our God, so to live that our daily conduct may reveal the beauty of our faith, and that the house of Israel may continue to give witness to Your truth among all people.
> (*ULPS* p143)

Ordination in a Thai Buddhist Monastery

If a person is trying to escape from suffering in the world it is pointless to turn to drugs or other sensual pleasures. Such escapes do not last and do not work. It is also pointless just getting depressed about it all. That doesn't solve anything either.

When Mike Dominski arrived in Thailand he was in search of an alternative to the frenzied pleasure seeking of the modern world.

Mike Dominski

For Mike, Buddhism offered what he was looking for; a way out of a world which seems obsessed with selfish greed.

After a few weeks at a Buddhist monastery in north east Thailand, Mike decided to go ahead with his plan to become a monk. He already was a Buddhist, now he decided to take his spiritual journey a stage further. The monastic path could be the best way to reach **Nirvana**. Buddhists believe that a person can become enlightened by following the Buddha's teaching and so be free of all the ignorance which fills our world.

THE ORDINATION CEREMONY

Before taking his monastic vows, Mike had to spend some time as a novice, preparing for ordination. He had to learn in Pali the 227 rules that Buddhist monks must keep. Pali is the language of the scriptures in the Thai Buddhist tradition (called Theravada). He also had to prepare by dyeing and sewing his own robes. At the ordination ceremony, Mike presented his robes and answered set questions to ensure his fitness for monastic life. Then he had to chant his ordination vows. Only if he said them perfectly would he be accepted as a monk.

The Venerable Punnadhammo Bhikkhu

It turned out fine, and Mike took on his new Buddhist name, 'Punnadhammo' which means 'Full of Truth and Wisdom'. 'A monk's life isn't for everyone,' says Punnadhammo, 'but for those with the right character it can be very fulfilling.'

THINGS TO DO

1 What sort of feelings might lead a person to try to escape from the modern world?

2 Buddhist monks take a vow of celibacy. Find out what this means, and why they do this. Discuss the idea in class.

3 What do you think will be better in Punnadhammo's new life? What do you think he will find most difficult?

4 Make up a name for a really good and holy person, like 'Full of Truth and Wisdom'.

10

KEEP IN TOUCH

Practice Makes Perfect

Having made a commitment to something, how do you keep it going? Some people seem to have powers of self-motivation and self-discipline which drive them to great heights of success. They have an aim and they stick to it.

Commonwealth Games Gold Medalist, Linford Christie, now in his thirties, has also won Olympic, European and World Championship golds. Yet at 25 he was not a serious contender. His main aim was to keep running for as long as he was doing well and giving entertainment and pleasure to his supporters.

Linford Christie

A surprise winner at the Commonwealth Games was Denise Lewis, a Wolverhampton secretary, who won the heptathlon gold. She owes her success partly to 'motivation classes' run by the British Athletic Federation and sports psychologist Alma Thomas. The classes helped Denise overcome her self-doubt.

'It's only once you start believing it's possible, that you can achieve it.'

Christie and Lewis have both had expert help from their coaches as well as support from friends and family. They have helped to bring out the best in them.

Denise Lewis

There are clues in the stories of athletic and sporting success to some of life's puzzles and mysteries. A sportsperson's period of success is very short, maybe 10 or 15 years if they're lucky. What will they do then? Remember the good old days for the next 50 years? Or use their mental toughness in other areas of life? Not every top athlete gets rich, but those who do often use their money to help others to get chances they might not have otherwise. Most top football teams, for example, support events to help handicapped children. Life, in other words, is more than sport.

THINGS TO DO

1 In pairs, debate the view that, in sport, 'it is the taking part, not the winning', which is most important.

2 Write down one skill you feel you could improve upon. What will you need to do?

3 Write a short story about a person who is helped by their beliefs to cope better with their ordinary life.

Daily Bread

To live life to the full, we need to keep bringing our aims to mind. Businesses, sports teams and schools keep reminding their members and clients of their goals, to keep them on task. Does your school have a motto or mission statement?

People who have committed themselves to a religious faith also have various means of keeping in touch with their beliefs and values, and keeping themselves on the right path. Here are examples from three religions:

REMEMBRANCE OF ALLAH

Muslims keep in touch with God by remembering his gifts and qualities throughout the day. As well as through set prayer (Salat), Muslims may call for God's help or blessing at any other time. For example:

Before meals: 'In the name of Allah, who sustains us and provides for us.'

After meals: 'All praise is due to Allah who has given us to eat and drink and has made us obedient to His will.'

Entering a building: 'O Lord, let my entry be by the Gate of Truth and Honour.' (17:81)

Before making a speech or taking part in a discussion: 'O my Lord, expand for me my breast, and ease my task for me, and remove the impediment from my speech, so they may understand what I say.' (20:26-29)

On taking medicine: 'In the name of Allah; He is the Healer.'

NAM JAPNA

For Sikhs, the development of their spiritual life is aided by the repetition of the name of God (Nam). This is not simply mindless repetition, but actually making God a part of the person in everything they do.

Guru Nanak said:

> 'Meditating on the True Name you shall find bliss in the palace of God.' (AG 689)

This practice of God remembrance helps the fight against evil and is known as Nam japna or Nam simran.

> 'Nam gives form to everything, Through Nam comes all wisdom and light.' (AG 986)

THE LORD'S PRAYER

Christians are reminded of the way of Jesus by daily recitation of the Lord's Prayer:

> Our Father in heaven
> May your holy name be honoured;
> may your kingdom come;
> may your will be done on earth as it is in heaven.
> Give us today the food we need.
> Forgive us the wrongs we have done,
> as we forgive the wrongs that others have done to us.
> Do not bring us to hard testing,
> but keep us safe from the Evil One.
> (Matthew 6:9-13)

THINGS TO DO

1 Choose one of the sentences from the religious teaching or prayers on this page. Make a decorative poster of your sentence for the classroom.

2 How do you feel about your school's motto/mission statement? Should it be repeated before every lesson?

The Grace of God

PSALM 22

My God, my God, why have you abandoned
me?

I have cried desperately for help,
but still it does not come.
During the day I call to you, my God,
but you do not answer . . .
But I am no longer a man; I am a worm,
despised and scorned by everyone.
All who see me jeer at me,
they stick out their tongues and shake their
heads
'You relied on the Lord,' they say,
'Why doesn't he save you?
If the Lord likes you,
why doesn't he help you?' . . .
I will tell my people what you have done;
I will praise you in their assembly:
'Praise him, you servants of the LORD!
Honour him, you descendants of Jacob!
Worship him, you people of Israel!
He does not neglect the poor or ignore their
suffering
he does not turn away from them,
but answers when they call for help . . .'

Despite the fact that the whole world seems to be
against the writer of this poem, he has not given up
his belief that, in the end, God will triumph. Prayers
and poems like this have sustained Jewish men and
women during times of hardship and persecution
through the centuries.

THINGS TO DO

1 Describe the feelings of the writer of Psalm 22
both at the beginning and the end of the
poem.

2 Look up Psalm 23. What are the feelings of
the writer this time?

3 Why do Christians also identify with these
two Psalms?

The Promised Land

Although he had led the Hebrews from slavery to freedom, Moses himself did not reach the Promised Land. He saw the land where his people were to settle from a hill top, but died before they got there.

A person's spiritual progress over a lifetime can be likened to the Hebrews' journey to the Promised Land. There are plenty of things to put you off on the way. Maybe a life of slavery seems better than the hardships which go with freedom!

People on such spiritual quests usually need help in keeping in touch with their vision. For most this will mean some kind of regular meeting with others who are on the same spiritual path as them. For Jewish people today that means attending a synagogue.

The Old Synagogue, Prague

THE MOSQUE

Muslims can pray wherever they are. A clean prayer mat can make any place ready for the worship of Allah. Many Muslims will have a room in their house where prayer can take place, but when they can, and especially on Fridays, they will attend a mosque (**masjid** in Arabic). A mosque is not just a place of prayer. It is also a meeting place and a place of rest for visitors or those on a long journey. The Imam (teacher) for the local community may give a sermon on the meaning of a part of the Qur'an. There may be rooms in the mosque for children to do Arabic and qur'anic studies and for celebrations connected with weddings, births and so on. In this way, Muslims keep in touch with religion and their ideals and values.

The Central Mosque, Cairo

THINGS TO DO

1   What modern films do you know that describe a journey and a quest?

2   How does attendance at a place of worship help the believer to keep in touch with their spiritual quest?

3   Divide the class up to investigate the different religious meeting places.